AF270375

HIGH-STAKES HEISTS

JEWEL HEISTS

KENNY ABDO

Fly!
An Imprint of Abdo Zoom
abdobooks.com

abdobooks.com

Published by Abdo Zoom, a division of ABDO, P.O. Box 398166, Minneapolis, Minnesota 55439. Copyright © 2025 by Abdo Consulting Group, Inc. International copyrights reserved in all countries. No part of this book may be reproduced in any form without written permission from the publisher. Fly!™ is a trademark and logo of Abdo Zoom.

Printed in the United States of America, North Mankato, Minnesota.
052024
092024

Photo Credits: AP Images, Getty Images, Shutterstock
Production Contributors: Kenny Abdo, Jennie Forsberg, Grace Hansen
Design Contributors: Candice Keimig, Neil Klinepier

Library of Congress Control Number: 2023948549

Publisher's Cataloging-in-Publication Data

Names: Abdo, Kenny, author.
Title: Jewel heists / by Kenny Abdo
Description: Minneapolis, Minnesota : Abdo Zoom, 2025 | Series: High-stakes heists | Includes online resources and index.
Identifiers: ISBN 9781098285739 (lib. bdg.) | ISBN 9781098286439 (ebook) | ISBN 9781098286781 (Read-to-me eBook)
Subjects: LCSH: Theft--Juvenile literature. | Jewelry theft--Juvenile literature. | Jewel thieves--Juvenile literature. | Stealing--Juvenile literature. | Robbery--Juvenile literature.
Classification: DDC 364.162--dc23

TABLE OF CONTENTS

JEWEL HEISTS

It has been said that jewelry can tell a story without a single word. But some criminals have written history with the precious stones and metals they have stolen!

THE
PLOTTING

Gemstones are precious rocks and **minerals** formed naturally by the earth. It takes time, pressure, and high temperatures to create them. Precious metals, such as gold and silver, are also made naturally.

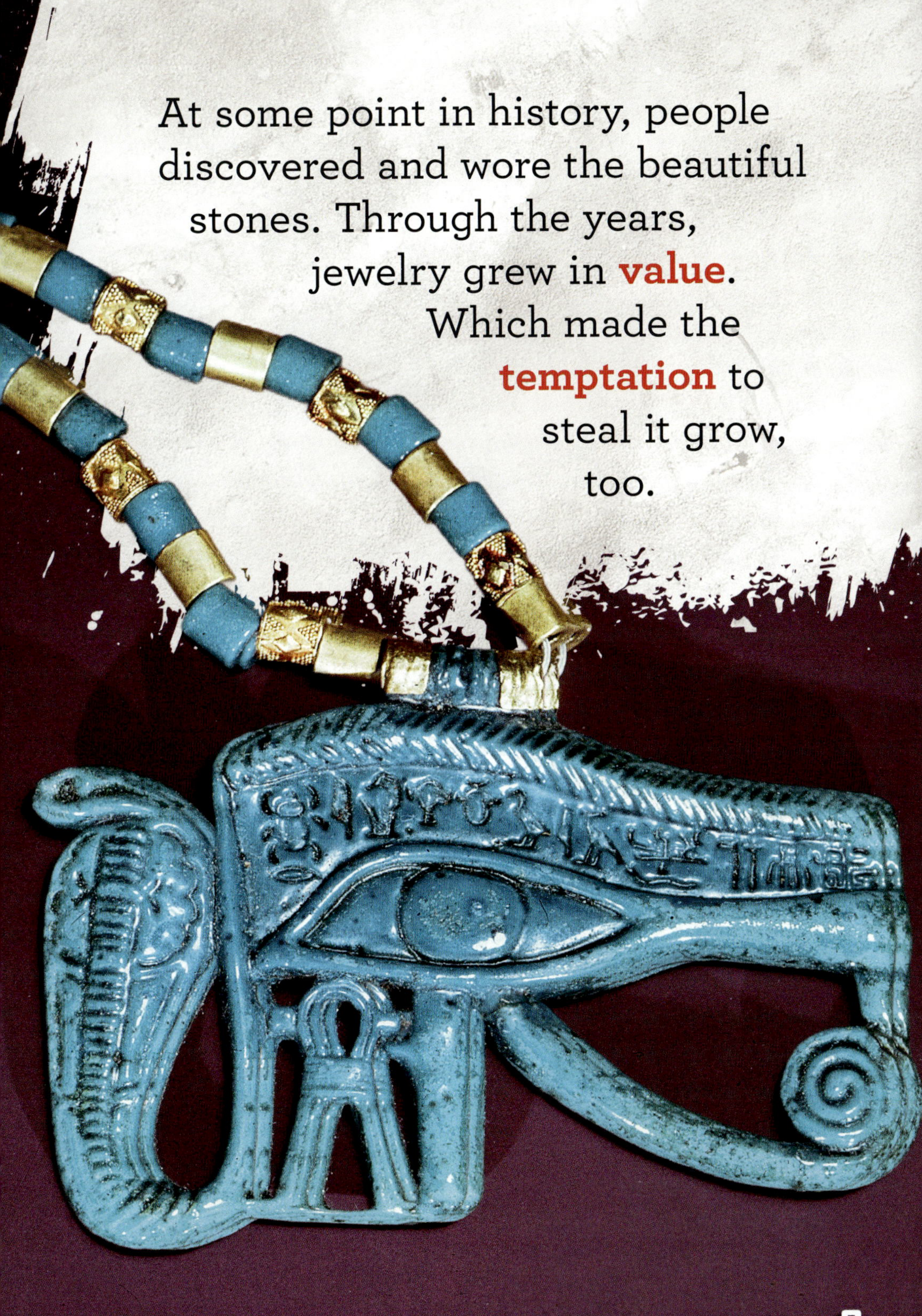

At some point in history, people discovered and wore the beautiful stones. Through the years, jewelry grew in **value**. Which made the **temptation** to steal it grow, too.

THE SCORES

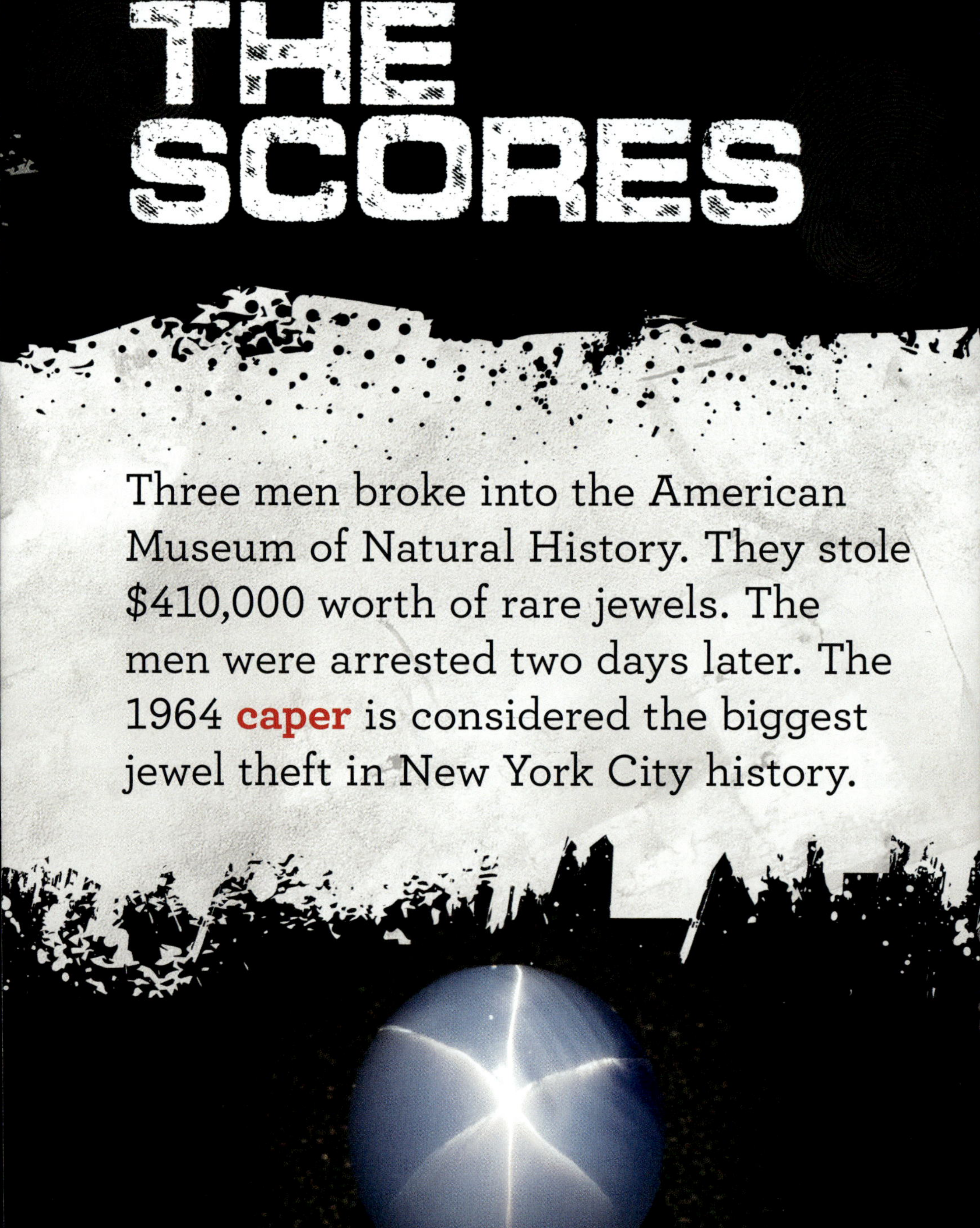

Three men broke into the American Museum of Natural History. They stole $410,000 worth of rare jewels. The men were arrested two days later. The 1964 **caper** is considered the biggest jewel theft in New York City history.

In 1983 in London, England, robbers broke into the Brink's-Mat warehouse. With the help of a security guard, the thieves took $41 million in gold. The gold was never recovered.

CARLTON
loree Rodkin
POLICE
Panasonic

The Carlton Hotel in Cannes, France, had the worst luck. In 1994, diamond thieves walked away with $60 million in loot. The same happened 19 years later. But this time, a single thief scored more than $130 million in jewelry!

A team of crooks broke into the underground vault of the Antwerp World Diamond Centre in Belgium. They took more than $100 million in diamonds! The 2003 heist is considered one of the biggest on record.

In 2005, four men approached the Schiphol Airport dressed as employees. They robbed an armored truck carrying $72 million in uncut **gems**. They were arrested in 2019. Only $43 million from the score was recovered.

Thieves drilled a tunnel to break into the Damiani Showroom in Milan, Italy, in 2008. They tied up the staff and got away with millions in gold, diamonds, and **emeralds**.

Two men pulled one of the largest jewelry heists in British history. They entered Graff Diamonds wearing face **prosthetics** and **nabbed** $65 million worth of jewelry. However, they left their phone in the getaway car, helping officials identify them.

Eight men disguised as police officers entered the Brussels Airport in Belgium looking for an airplane filled with diamonds. In just three minutes, the group snatched $50 million worth of the precious stones. In 2013, 31 people were arrested in connection with the robbery.

Doge's Palace in Venice, Italy, was robbed in broad daylight in 2018. Thieves managed to delay the security alarm by one minute. It was enough time to **flee** without attracting attention.

THE GETAWAY

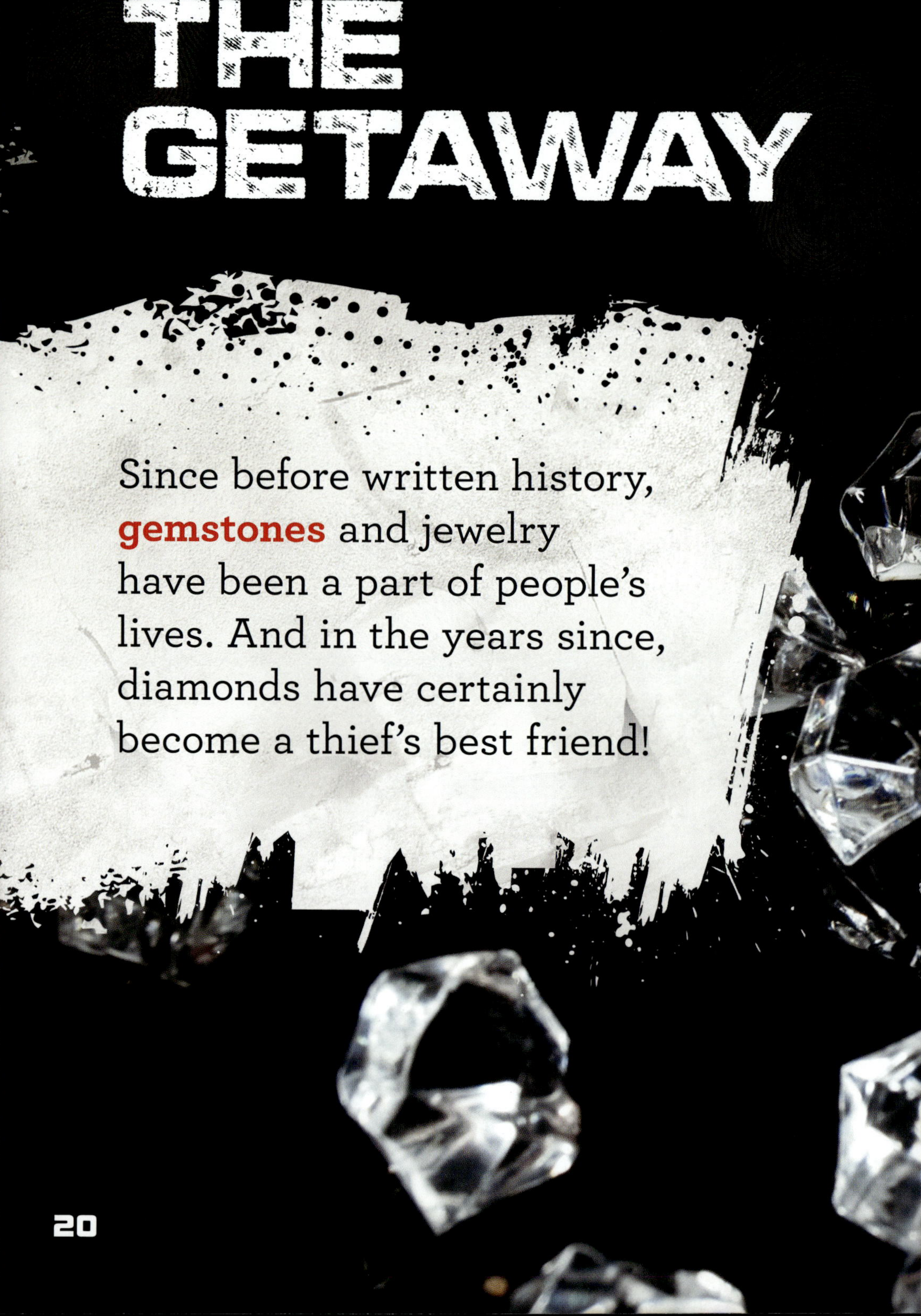

Since before written history, **gemstones** and jewelry have been a part of people's lives. And in the years since, diamonds have certainly become a thief's best friend!

GLOSSARY

caper – a planned criminal activity.

emerald – a clear green stone that is used in jewelry.

flee – to quickly run away or escape.

gemstone – a valuable stone such as an emerald or a diamond, cut and polished for jewelry.

mineral – a substance formed in the earth that is not of an animal or a plant.

nabbed – grabbed, snatched, or stolen.

prosthetics – make-up and or rubber pieces that transforms a person's face to look different.

temptation – the act or an instance of tempting, or the condition of being tempted.

valued – the amount of money that something is worth.

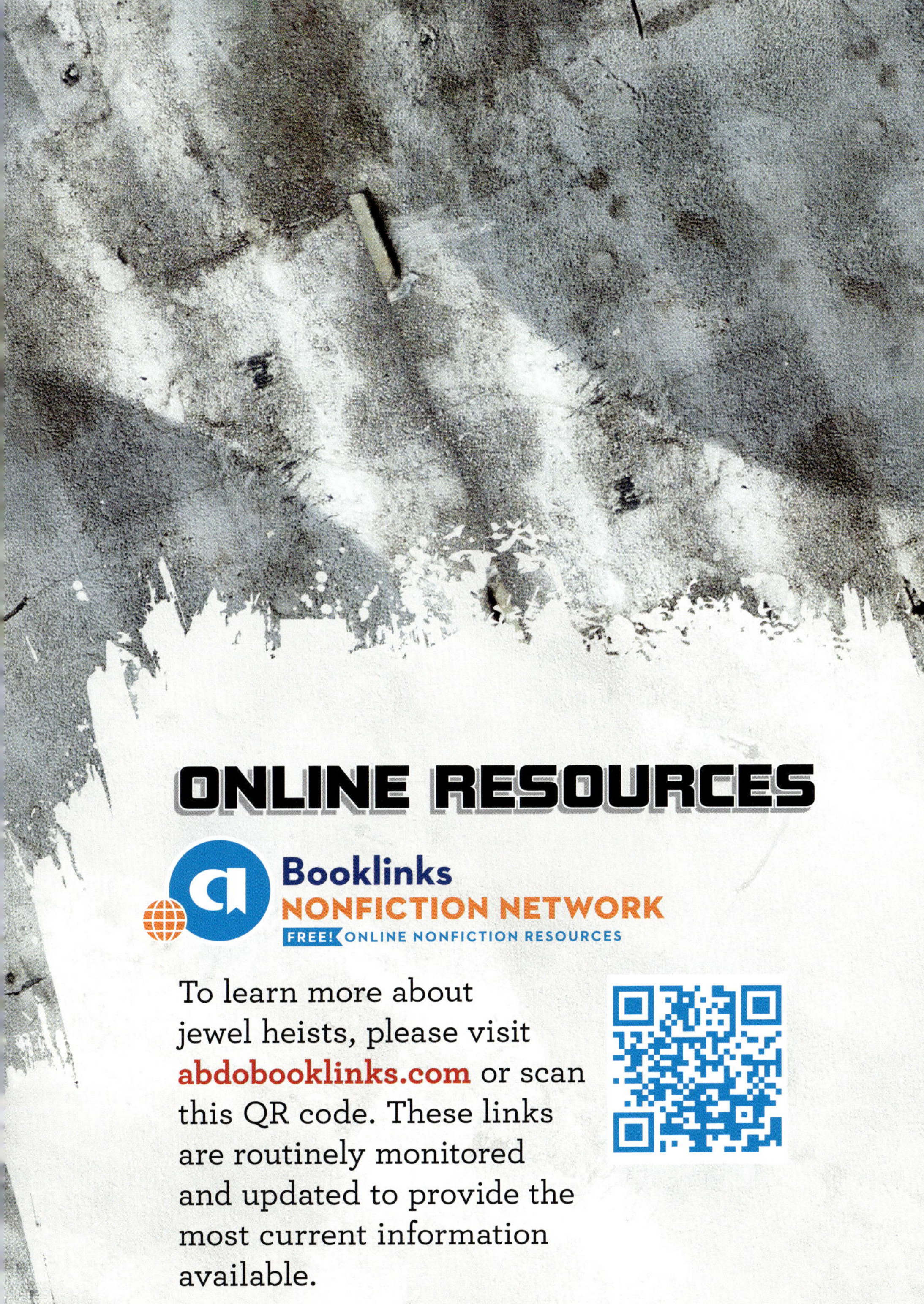
ONLINE RESOURCES

Booklinks
NONFICTION NETWORK
FREE! ONLINE NONFICTION RESOURCES

To learn more about
jewel heists, please visit
abdobooklinks.com or scan
this QR code. These links
are routinely monitored
and updated to provide the
most current information
available.

INDEX